scones

by Genevieve Knights

WKP

www.**scones**.co.nz

Contents

About the Author

Genevieve Knights is an Auckland, New Zealand-based chef, food writer and food photographer. She began her culinary career, spanning 20 years as an apprentice chef in 1990. Her motto from the beginning has been to gain the best experience possible working for those at the top of their game in hospitality. Her resumé includes restaurants and catering establishments of iconic status such as The French Café, Wheeler's Restaurant, Veranda Bar and Grill, Austin's Catering and Mantells of Mt Eden.

Genevieve took on her first executive chef role at the age of 23 in a small café, and later again at the age of 28 under the guidance of well-known chef, restaurant owner and mentor Dominique Parat. In the years that followed she discovered a passion for food and recipe writing. The website "Genevieve's Cuisine" was brought to life in 2004, followed shortly after by the Penguin-published book *Basic But Brilliant* in 2005.

In creating the website and her two cookbooks, Genevieve has cut her teeth in food photography and continues to write and photograph food and recipes that promote branded products. Her food writing has been published in *Cuisine, Foodtown Magazine, The Parnell Darling* and *New Zealand Golf Magazine*. She publishes a foodie calendar annually for Saint Publishing and was featured in the celebrity chef cookbook *East Meets West*, the proceeds of which were donated to tsunami relief.

Genevieve's television experience has included working as an itinerant presenter and chef for the TV show "Good Morning" and co-presenting TVCs for Masterfoods. She lives with her husband and business partner Wayne Knights in the suburb of Parnell in Auckland's central business district. *Scones* is their first joint project under the White Knights Publishing banner.

Acknowledgement

I would like to thank my husband Wayne for his never-ending support in all my creative endeavours.

This book would not have been possible without his tireless work ethic, terrific graphic design skills and tenacity.

Collaborating on *scones* has been a magical journey that I'm sure will continue far into our future together.

Scones in History

An oblong block of red sandstone called *The Stone of Destiny* – also known as *The Stone of Scone*, *Jacob's Pillow* or *The Coronation Stone* – used in the coronation of Scottish kings, was kept in an abbey in the city of Scone (near Perth). It is still used in British coronations to this day but resides at Edinburgh Castle between ceremonies. However, the first mention of the edible scone – or *sconnis* – was made by Scottish poet Gavin Douglas around 1513. The word is likely derived from Middle Dutch ("schoonbrot") or Middle German ("schonbrot"), meaning "fine white bread". While it is probable the scone had been around for some time before this date, due to illiteracy few recipes were written down. Originally an unleavened griddle cake or quick bread – a small plate-size round cake cooked on a griddle then cut into wedges to serve – in the mid-nineteenth century bicarbonate of soda became widely available and scones were made with sour milk or buttermilk then baked in the oven or on a griddle.

The history of modern baking powder begins in the mid-eighteenth century. In order for baking powder to work, an alkali and acid need to react with one another. The first version of this kind of leavening can be traced back to Central America where an alkali was made by leaching wood ashes. This was called pearlash and worked when mixed into a flour-based cake provided an acid was present to set off the leavening reaction. Classic early examples of the acidic ingredients are gingerbread using molasses and cornbread that uses buttermilk. The problem was that the reaction began as soon as the ingredients mixed, meaning you had to get the cake in the oven to bake as quickly as possible. Gradually, baking sodas became a popular replacement for pearlash, which can react with the fats in foods making them taste soapy. Soda has the same reaction but to a much lesser extent.

Soon it became apparent that an alkali and an acid could be mixed together to create the first baking powders. This way, acidic ingredients in the recipe were no longer required for leavening. Cream of tartar, otherwise known as tartaric acid, was mixed with baking soda, both of which conveniently form crystals. Unfortunately, this mix reacts with wheat flour as soon as it becomes wet, once again giving little time to prepare and cook the dough before leavening stops. These days, some of the tartaric acid in baking powder has been replaced with sodium pyrophosphate, which is slow to react and requires heat for a full reaction. In addition, most baking powders have two leaveners. One reacts with liquids while another reacts with heat. That way, baking gets a double boost, making a recipe more reliable.

Leaching wood ashes in the days of old would have taken an impressive amount of effort compared to nipping down to a food store to buy flour and baking powder! So thanks to the ingredients that have been developed over the centuries, we can now bake whatever scone flavour takes our fancy. This was in fact the inspiration for my book. Typically, scones are mostly eaten plain topped with butter and jam, and while cheese scones are likewise a popular staple in cafés, there are precious few alternative flavours on offer, leading me to ask myself: Why is this ancient and venerable recipe so rarely given a modern twist?

I believe the reason to be that the basic recipe has people constantly striving to perfect its simple yet tricky technique, with so many failures that friendly but intense competition has developed between home bakers – almost to the point where if you don't succeed after a couple of tries, you feel that you may as well give up and choose to brag about the best scones in the world your gran used to make instead!

So,
in order to inspire
because it may have been a mystery prior,
from the history of what was once cooked over a fire,
to a modern-day version to which you can aspire,
I'll prove you can even put them in a deep-fryer!
Now you too can make scones for all to admire....

Oh, and please read the "Scone Secrets" section first so that my promises can transpire!

Scone Secrets

Many people struggle with the basics of making scones. The recipes seem so simple and straight-forward in theory, yet there are a number of factors involved in ensuring you get a good result.

The recipes

Interestingly, there are many types of traditional scone that didn't make it into this book. For instance, where are the potato scones? I attempted variation after variation of potato scones and just didn't feel the reader would enjoy the results as much as other recipes that *are* included. In fact, almost as many recipes were rejected as made the cut.

While lemonade (fizzy drink) scones are in, they are in fact so similar to cream scones made with 50/50 cream and water that you would be hard pressed to tell the difference. And though milk is considered the classic liquid ingredient in a scone, the results can be so much better with the use of other dairy products you may have never considered before.

In selecting a recipe to try, the introductions will help you decide which type of scone will suit your taste. Traditional, dainty, or *off the charts unique* ideas have all been compiled to cater for a diversity of tastes. Bear in mind, too, that the recipes in these pages make a small quantity of scones – enough for 4 to 6 people depending on what type of meal is being served. If you are baking for more, the quantities will need to be increased accordingly.

Flour & raising agents

Most people equate scone making with self-raising flour, but you will notice that most of my recipes use standard flour and baking powder rather than self-raising. It is my own experience that self-raising flour is more likely to begin leavening before the scones are placed in the oven.

The baking powders we buy today have double leaveners. One reacts with liquids and another reacts with heat. That way, baking gets a double boost and makes a recipe more reliable. Stabilisers are added to ensure the main amount of leavening occurs with the application of heat. Self-raising flour is a combination of flour and baking powder, so why this should happen beforehand is a mystery but certainly not a disaster. Your scones will still work using either flour; and over-kneading is a more likely cause of flat scones.

However, bearing in mind that raising agents can activate before heat is applied, never leave dough sitting on the bench for too long before shaping and baking. Make sure your oven is preheated before beginning the recipe. Once the liquid is applied, shape the dough immediately and bake for the best results.

Sifting

Sifting is not necessary but can be helpful to aerate and combine the dry ingredients. It is particularly important when using spices so as to avoid intensely flavoured lumps in your scones.

Fat content

The classic combination of fat and liquid in scones is milk and butter. But some dairy products – such as yoghurt, sour cream, crème fraîche, and mascarpone – can replace both ingredients. The main difference with the scone dough made of other dairy products is that it is much softer to work with. The results are fantastic, though, with soft, melt-in-your-mouth scones that cut out the process of rubbing in the butter thus making even shorter work of an already quick-to-make recipe.

Most cheese scones have butter rubbed in, but I mainly omitted this step as I deem it unnecessary to the end result. There is plenty of fat in a cheese scone without adding more butter. The cheese, however, needs to be grated very finely for even distribution through the flour. It is even possible to rub cheese into the flour if it is too soft to grate, as with blue cheese.

The big exception to the rule is one of my very favourite recipes for Sour Cream Griddle Scones. Sour cream and butter are needed for the ultimate result. I may only eat them once a year, but like me, you will be amazed at how light in texture they are with all the extra decadent ingredients.

On a "liter" note, you can substitute low-fat yoghurt to moisten the dry ingredients without butter. The scones work out okay but can be a little lacking in flavour and tend to be a bit dry in texture. However, this is preferable to never eating scones because they contain fattening dairy products.

We tend to forget that scones are in fact a quick bread or soda bread, and like regular bread can be made with vegetable oils instead of butter. The result is, of course, bread-like, but considering the short amount of time it takes to make soda bread compared to regular bread, it's well worth a go.

Combining dry & wet ingredients

When making scones, the technique of combining the wet and dry ingredients is possibly the most crucial factor in how your scones will turn out. The reason for this is the gluten content in flour. When wheat flour dough is kneaded, the gluten strands stretch, toughening its structure. If such dough is leavened with yeast, as with bread, sugar fermentation produces bubbles of carbon dioxide which, trapped by the gluten network, cause the dough to swell or rise. More kneading leads to chewier products like pizza and bagels, while less kneading yields tender baked goods.

Shortening or fat helps to hinder the stretching of gluten strands, so it is used, along with minimal working, when tender baked goods such as scones are desired. Even 3 or 4 extra kneads can lead to scones half as high as they could have been.

For the best results, make sure your wet ingredients are either mixed together or added at the same time. The main aim is to mix the ingredients the least amount possible before they are rolled out. I find a fork best for mixing the wet and dry ingredients together without overworking parts of the dough, which you can risk if using a metal or wooden spoon.

Never add all the wet ingredients in one go. Instead, add half then drizzle in the rest until achieving a moist enough consistency for dough to form. Due to the difference in flours from brand to brand and country to country, it is better not to assume you will require all the liquid in each recipe.

Kneading

It isn't possible to stress enough how important it is not to overwork the dough once the ingredients are combined. When enough liquid has been added but before it forms one lump, tip onto a lightly floured surface.

Making sure the different-sized clods are evenly moist, work them gently together. The dough doesn't have to be kneaded until smooth. It is better to have a rough texture on the surface than risk a flat scone. Rolling out will also help the ingredients to meld, so don't feel you need the dough to be totally combined before you begin working on it with the rolling pin.

Baking

"You bake it until it's cooked", as my grandmother used to say. Back in the day of coal ranges, women were so used to baking at home, they could smell when something was ready to come out of the oven from the other end of the house.

While the odd divine whiff comes my way in a similar fashion, I don't trust myself enough to bake anything at home without a timer. My suggestion is to set the timer for three quarters of the baking time, then reset it for every couple of minutes after that. Perfect results every time!

Serving

Scones should be served on the day they are baked. There are many serving suggestions included in the introductions throughout the book, but don't feel limited to these. Scones containing liquor-soaked fruit in particular should be eaten before they have cooled to room temperature if the full flavour is to be enjoyed. They are great for occasions like Christmas and the ingredients can be weighed out ready to be mixed for minimal fuss while you entertain family and guests.

Savoury scones go really well with soups – for example, the Dill and Crème Fraîche Scones would pair well with seafood chowder. Try scones as canapés cut small and topped with your favourite toppings. Be sure to try the Beer & Cheddar Bites cut larger with dips and spreads, or the Mini Cheese Burger and Sausage Scones for casual or kids' parties. The Scone Pizza and Bacon & Egg Scone Slice can also be cut small for party hand-arounds.

Sweet scones are not limited to high tea or morning tea – try them as a dessert with ice cream and sweet sauces. The griddle scones are a must-try for breakfast or brunch, and mini scones can make the cutest petit fours you have ever seen. My favourite is the Rich Dark Chocolate Scones topped with softened piped chocolate ganache.

While they do freeze, a thawed scone is not of the same quality. However, day-old scones, especially cheese flavoured, can be microwaved quite hot to a reasonable standard and it's certainly preferable to disposal.

Creativity with recipes

There are 50 scone recipes presented in this book, but that doesn't mean there aren't numerous other possible flavour variations to make. For example, there's no reason the wholemeal scone recipe can't be used in a pinwheel, and likewise the dairy-free dough can be used in every variation that doesn't contain cheese or another dairy product. The recipes are a guideline only, providing a convenient starting point for your own imagination and personal taste to take flight.

Savoury Scone Recipes

Bacon & Egg Scone Slice

Inspired by the Kiwi classic bacon and egg pie, this slice takes only a fraction of the time to prepare, making it a very practical dish. Be extra diligent to ensure the rim won't leak any egg for the best results.

200g plain flour
2 teaspoons baking powder
¼ teaspoon salt
200–250mls double cream
6 rashers bacon, fried until crisp
4 eggs

Preheat the oven to 200°C. Sift the flour, baking powder and salt together into a medium-sized mixing bowl. Add 200mls of cream then work in with a fork until you have even-sized-looking clumps. If the mix is too dry, add the remaining 50mls cream.

Place on a floured workbench and knead a couple of times. Roll the dough out to a 25cm square and place on a lightly floured baking tray. Trim the sides to form an even square. Fold over the edges to create a small rim that won't leak any egg. Chop the bacon roughly and sprinkle over the dough. Crack the eggs evenly over the bacon. Pierce the yolks so they run. Bake for 12–15 minutes until the egg has cooked through. To serve, slice into 9 even squares.

Makes 9 squares

Spinach, Feta & Black Olive Pinwheels

These tasty pinwheels are practically a meal in themselves. They are quick and easy to prepare and are great to take to the beach for picnics. Or you could try them for brunch served hot from the oven with crispy bacon and poached eggs.

200g plain flour

2 teaspoons baking powder

¼ teaspoon salt

150g feta

20 calamata olives, pitted and sliced

120mls water

3 large handfuls baby spinach leaves

milled black pepper

sea salt flakes

Preheat the oven to 220°C. Line a baking tray with non-stick baking paper. Sift the flour, baking powder and salt into a medium-sized mixing bowl. Crumble in the feta and add the olives. Pour over the water then stir to combine with a fork. Knead lightly into a dough – you may need to add a little extra water if the mix is too dry.

Place the dough on a lightly floured surface. Roll out to a rectangle roughly 40cm x 25cm. Place the dough on the bench so the 40cm length is horizontal. Sprinkle the dough evenly with the spinach leaves. Season with milled black pepper and sea salt flakes. Brush the far edge lightly with water. Roll up from the front to the back. Press lightly to make sure the sticky edge secures the roll. Slice the roll 2cm apart. Place slices cut side up onto the baking tray. Bake for 6–8 minutes until lightly browned.

Makes 12

Mini Poppy Seed Dampers

The original Australian damper is a plain recipe of flour, soda, buttermilk and salt. In this recipe, I have made the dampers miniature and substituted Greek yoghurt for the buttermilk. Yoghurt gives dough a soft and airy artisan bread-like texture, and when topped with poppy seeds you have an instant bread roll.

400g plain flour

4 teaspoons baking powder

½ teaspoon salt

milled black pepper

30mls extra virgin olive oil

200g thick Greek yoghurt

150mls milk

4 tablespoons poppy seeds

softened cream cheese

tomato

Preheat the oven to 200°C. Line a baking tray with non-stick baking paper. Sift the flour, baking powder and salt into a medium-sized mixing bowl. Add a good grind of milled black pepper. With a fork, work in the olive oil. Add the Greek yoghurt and milk then stir to combine.

Turn the dough out onto a floured workbench. Knead together until the dough is smooth. Cut the dough into 8 even pieces. Shape into round balls. Roll the top of the dough balls in the poppy seeds then place on the baking tray. Make 2 cuts in a cross pattern on top of the dough. Bake for 15–20 minutes until they turn golden brown and sound hollow when tapped. When cool, slice in half and fill with cream cheese and tomato slices.

Makes 8

Sausage Scones

This recipe transforms a cabanossi sausage into a tasty sausage roll that is ready to eat in minutes. There is also much less fat in this recipe compared with the original puff pastry sausage roll. Serve them piping hot and fresh out of the oven with plenty of tomato ketchup on the side.

200g plain flour

2 teaspoons baking powder

½ teaspoon salt

50g butter

1 tablespoon mild or hot English mustard

100–120mls milk

4 small frankfurters

Preheat the oven to 220°C. Line a baking tray with non-stick baking paper. Place the flour, baking powder and salt into a medium-sized mixing bowl. Rub in the butter until the texture resembles fine breadcrumbs. Separately whisk together the mustard and milk. Add most of the milk and mustard to the dry mix. With a fork, stir to combine. If the mix is too dry to come together, add the remaining milk.

Transfer to a lightly floured surface and knead the dough together. Roll the dough out to a 30cm x 20cm rectangle. Place the dough on the bench so the 20cm width is in front of you. Slice dough into 4 even pieces across the width. Place a frankenfurter at the edge of a dough rectangle and brush the farthest edge with a little water. Roll up tightly then press lightly to secure. Repeat the process with the other frankenfurters. Slice the rolls into 5 even pieces each and place them onto the baking tray so they sit on the pastry join. Bake 6–8 minutes until golden brown.

Makes 20

Goat's Cheese & Sage Scones

If you love goat's cheese as much as I do, this could well be your favourite recipe in this book. Goat's cheese and sage scones are the perfect luncheon item smeared with cream cheese or softened feta.

200g plain flour
2 teaspoons bicarbonate of soda
½ teaspoon salt
200g goat's cheese or goat's feta
1 small handful sage leaves
milled black pepper
200mls buttermilk

Preheat the oven to 220°C. Line a baking tray with non-stick baking paper. In a medium-sized mixing bowl, sift in the flour, bicarbonate of soda and salt. Crumble in the goat's cheese. Roughly chop the sage leaves and add to the bowl along with a good grind of milled black pepper. Add the buttermilk and stir to combine with a fork.

Tip the dough onto a lightly floured surface and knead a couple of times to bring the dough together. Dust with flour then roll into a log around 4cm wide. Flatten log slightly then cut into 3cm slices. Place on the baking tray cut side up and bake for 6–8 minutes until golden brown and cooked through.

Makes 15

Beer & Cheddar Bites

Moreish beer and cheddar bites make a great afternoon snack over beers for spectator TV sports, BBQs and party snacks. The recipe makes enough bites for 4–6 people, so if you have a group coming over, double or triple this recipe and beware… they still won't last long!

200g self-raising flour
¼ teaspoon salt
1 small pinch chilli powder
80g cheddar cheese
120–140mls beer

Preheat oven to 220°C. Sift the flour, salt and chilli powder into a medium-sized mixing bowl. Grate the cheese on the fine side of a grater and add to the bowl. With a fork, stir in enough beer to form dough.

Pour the mix out onto a floured workbench and knead until the dough just comes together. Dust again with flour and roll the mix flat with a rolling pin to 1cm thick. Cut out 3cm circles with a crimped cookie cutter and place on a lightly floured baking tray. Knead the offcuts gently back together and repeat the rolling and cutting process. Bake for 6–8 minutes until golden brown.

Makes 25

Ham & Mustard Pinwheels

These savoury pinwheels make for a tasty lunch, brunch or picnic. You can also add your favourite cheese! After placing on the ham, sprinkle with the grated cheese of your choice and roll up as per the instructions for a ham, cheese and mustard pinwheel.

200g plain flour

2 teaspoons baking powder

½ teaspoon salt

2 tablespoons whole seed mustard

200g sour cream

60mls water

250g sliced ham

Preheat the oven to 220°C and line a baking tray with non-stick baking paper. Sift the flour, baking powder and salt into a medium-sized mixing bowl. Add the mustard and sour cream then stir to combine with a fork. Drizzle with the water then knead lightly into dough. Place the dough on a lightly floured surface. Roll out to a rectangle roughly 40cm x 25cm.

Place the dough on the bench so the 40cm length is horizontal. Cover the dough with the ham slices. Brush the far edge lightly with water. Roll up, rolling from the front to the back. Press lightly to make sure the sticky edge secures the roll. Slice into 12 even pieces. Place slices cut side up onto the baking tray. Bake for 6–8 minutes until lightly browned.

Makes 12

Walnut Scones

This is my version of a savoury cream cracker to enjoy with a cheeseboard. While you can enjoy all cheeses with walnut scones, it pairs ideally with blue. The nutty crunch and wholemeal texture complements the smooth cream flavour and salty richness of blue cheese best.

120g plain flour

2 teaspoons baking powder

½ teaspoon salt

80g wholemeal flour

2 tablespoons quality Parmesan, grated fine

70g walnuts

200mls double cream

water

Preheat the oven to 220°C. Sift the plain flour, baking powder and salt into a medium-sized mixing bowl. Add the wholemeal flour and Parmesan. Chop the walnuts roughly and add to the bowl. With a fork, stir in the cream. Add a drizzle of water if the mix is too dry to come together, and then knead minimally to form dough.

Roll dough out onto a lightly floured surface to half a centimetre thick. Using a crimped 4cm circle cutter, cut circles from the mix and place on a lightly floured baking tray. Knead dough back together and repeat the process. Bake for 4–6 minutes until lightly browned and cooked through.

Makes 25

Mascarpone & Chive Griddle Scones

These creamy savoury griddle scones make a great addition to a breakfast or brunch. Serve in place of toast or hash browns with bacon, eggs and fried tomatoes, or just on their own with soft butter.

200g plain flour

2 teaspoons baking powder

½ teaspoon salt

2 tablespoons fresh chopped chives

250g mascarpone

100–120mls milk

Place a large cast-iron pan onto a medium heat. Sift the flour, baking powder and salt into a medium-sized mixing bowl. Add the chives and mascarpone, then work in with a fork. Add the milk a little at a time until the mix comes together to form a dough – you may not need all the milk.

On a floured surface, knead the dough 2 or 3 times. Divide into 12 even pieces then pat each piece into a flat circle around half a centimetre thick. In 2 batches, place the dough circles into the hot dry pan. Turn over after 2 minutes then cook a further 2 minutes. Keep warm in the oven until serving time.

Serves 4

Blue Cheese & Sunflower Seed Scones

These full-of-fibre scones are very flavourful but the greatest thing about them is the texture the seeds and bran give them. The strength of the blue cheese will determine how strong the blue cheese flavour will be, so use blue brie for mild and Stilton for extra strong, though any kind of blue cheese will work well.

100g plain flour

100g bran

2½ teaspoons baking powder

½ teaspoon salt

100g blue cheese

100g sunflower seeds

150mls milk

Preheat the oven to 220°C. Place the flour, bran, baking powder and salt into a medium-sized mixing bowl and stir together. Crumble in the blue cheese then rub in with your fingers as you would butter until you have the consistency of fine breadcrumbs. Add the sunflower seeds and milk. With a fork, stir to combine then work into a dough with your hand. You may need a little water to moisten the dough if it is too dry.

Place the dough on a lightly floured surface and roll into a log 5cm wide. With a large sharp knife, cut 12 slices on an angle to create ovals. Place on a lightly floured baking tray cut side up and bake 6–8 minutes until lightly browned and cooked through.

Makes 12

Cornbread Scones

An easy version of cornbread, these scones are great as a light lunch or brunch item. Serve them with toppings like cream cheese, softened feta (as pictured), cured meats, pickles and slices of fresh tomato.

150g plain flour

2 teaspoons bicarbonate of soda

½ teaspoon salt

100g butter

1 tablespoon ground cumin

100g fine ground cornmeal

200mls buttermilk

Preheat the oven to 220°C. Sift the flour, bicarbonate of soda and salt into a medium-sized mixing bowl. Dice the butter fine then rub into the flour until its consistency resembles fine breadcrumbs. Add the cumin and cornmeal. Stir in the buttermilk until just combined.

Tip dough onto a lightly floured surface and roll into an even log about 4cm wide. Slice into 12 pieces and place on a lightly floured baking tray cut side up. Bake for 6–8 minutes until lightly browned and cooked through.

Makes 12

Garlic Butter Scones

These delicious savoury scones will fill the house with the smell of garlic bread while they bake. The extra butter turns them beautifully brown in colour and gives a light, crisp texture reminiscent of puff pastry. Serve them as a lunch item or they are great still warm out of the oven, at a BBQ.

200g self-raising flour
½ teaspoon salt
50g butter
100g thick Greek yoghurt
60–80mls water
additional 50g butter at room temperature
1 tablespoon whole seed mustard
2 large garlic cloves, minced

Preheat the oven to 220°C. Line a baking tray with non-stick baking paper. Sift the flour and salt into a medium-sized mixing bowl. Rub in the butter until the flour has the consistency of fine breadcrumbs. Add the yoghurt and stir to combine with a fork. Stir in enough water to form dough. Knead lightly to bring together. Place the dough on a lightly floured surface. Roll out to a rectangle roughly 40cm x 25cm.

Place the dough on the bench so the 40cm length is horizontal. In a small bowl, stir together the additional 50g butter, mustard and garlic. With a spatula or palette knife, smooth the garlic butter evenly over the dough until it is completely covered. Holding the horizontal edge closest to you, fold to halfway and lightly press flat. Do the same with the farthest edge so they meet in the middle. Fold dough in half horizontally again and press gently to secure. Slice into 12 even slices across the width. Place the slices cut side up onto the baking tray. Bake for 6–8 minutes until golden brown.

Makes 12

Pumpkin & Parmesan Scones

Pumpkin scones have a very mild pumpkin flavour but they look amazing and have a soft yummy texture. Serve them up as an accompaniment to soft cheeses like Brie, blue and goat's cheese.

100g pumpkin, seeded and skinned

200g plain flour

2 teaspoons baking powder

½ teaspoon salt

80g quality grated Parmesan

100g pumpkin seeds

80–100mls double cream

Preheat the oven to 220°C. Place the pumpkin into a microwave-proof dish, cover and microwave on high for 8 minutes. Leave to cool to room temperature then mash. Sift the flour, baking powder and salt into a medium-sized mixing bowl. Add the cooled pumpkin, Parmesan, pumpkin seeds and cream. Using a fork, stir to combine. Place onto a lightly floured surface and knead a couple of times to work into dough.

Roll out to 1cm thick. Using a 5cm round cookie cutter, cut circles from the dough and place on a lightly floured baking tray. Knead back together any leftover dough and repeat the process. Bake for 6–8 minutes until golden brown.

Makes 20

Mini Cheese Burger Scones

Kids old and young love these!

200g plain flour

2 teaspoons baking powder

½ teaspoon salt

80g cheddar cheese, grated fine

120mls water

2 tablespoons sesame seeds

300g beef mince

lettuce leaves

tomato sauce

3 small tomatoes

cucumber

Preheat the oven to 220°C. Sift the flour, baking powder and salt into a medium-sized mixing bowl. With a fork, stir in the cheese and water. Add a drizzle more of water if the mix is too dry to come together, and then knead minimally to form dough.

Sprinkle dough well with sesame seeds then roll out onto a lightly floured surface to half a centimetre thick. Using a round 4cm cutter, cut circles from the mix and place on a lightly floured baking tray. Knead dough back together and repeat the process. Bake for 4–6 minutes until lightly browned and cooked through.

Roll meat into 15 small patties. Fry meat patties in a little oil until browned and cooked through. Cut the scones in half through the middle. Place lettuce onto the bases then place on the patties and tomato sauce. Place on tomato and cucumber slices then top with the scone lid. Secure with skewers and serve immediately.

Makes 12

Parmesan Pinwheels

This recipe is a modern and tasty take on the well-cherished cheese scone. Quality Parmesan is a necessity for the best results and you can substitute with other cheeses like cheddars or Brie. Parmesan pinwheels are the perfect item as part of a brunch or light lunch, or great with afternoon tea! You can dress them up with cream cheese and salami or just enjoy as is. For a light option, stick with Parmesan and use one of the buttermilk scone recipes without sugar.

200g plain flour

2 teaspoons baking powder

¼ teaspoon salt

200mls double cream

100g quality Parmesan, grated

1 tablespoon fresh thyme, chopped

milled black pepper and sea salt flakes

Preheat the oven to 220°C. Line a baking tray with non-stick baking paper. Sift the flour, baking powder and salt into a medium-sized mixing bowl. Pour over the cream then stir to combine with a fork. Knead lightly into a dough – you may need to add a little water if the mix is too dry. Place the dough on a lightly floured surface. Roll out to a rectangle roughly 40cm x 25cm.

Place the dough on the bench so the 40cm length is horizontal. Sprinkle the dough evenly with the grated Parmesan and thyme. Season with milled black pepper and sea salt flakes. Brush the far edge lightly with water. Roll up from the front to the back. Press lightly to make sure the sticky edge secures the roll. Slice the roll 2cm apart. Place slices cut side up onto the baking tray. Bake for 6–8 minutes until lightly browned.

Makes 14

Roast Garlic & Black Olive Damper

Dampers are an Australian, early settler version of scones. The recipe is basically the same as scones but they were cooked on a griddle or in cast-iron pots over an open fire. Dampers were also cooked in one piece as a quick bread to enjoy with anything from jam to sliced meat, or whatever was handy. You can enjoy this recipe as you would an olive focaccia, warm from the oven with lashings of aioli.

1 head of garlic

1 tablespoon soya bean oil

400g plain flour

4 teaspoons baking powder

½ teaspoon salt

60mls extra virgin olive oil

20 pitted and sliced calamata olives

1 tablespoon fresh rosemary, chopped roughly

200–250mls buttermilk

extra virgin olive oil for brushing

Preheat the oven to 200°C. Peel the garlic cloves and place in a small bowl. Toss with the canola oil. Wrap in foil like a flat parcel so the cloves sit in a single layer. Place on the bars of the oven and bake for 20 minutes.

Line a baking tray with non-stick baking paper and set aside. Sift the flour, baking powder and salt into a medium-sized mixing bowl. With a fork, mix in the olive oil. Mash the garlic slightly and add along with the sliced olives and rosemary. Add 200mls of the buttermilk then stir to combine with a fork. If the mix is too dry to form dough, add the remaining buttermilk.

Turn the dough out onto a floured workbench. Knead together until the dough is smooth. Shape into a large round then roll flat until it's around 20cm in diameter. Score 8 wedges lightly across the surface. Brush with extra olive oil. Bake for 15–20 minutes until golden brown and the loaf sounds hollow when tapped.

Serves 6

Scone Pizza

Scones are a member of the quick-bread family, so this is a recipe for pizza lovers in a big hurry who don't have time to prove yeast dough. You can use any of your favourite toppings with this recipe but try not to load the toppings too high to ensure a crisp base.

200g self-raising flour
½ teaspoon salt
30mls extra virgin olive oil
150mls warm water
50g pizza sauce
16 slices pepperoni
8 large pimento stuffed queen green olives
4 balls bocconcini (fresh mozzarella balls)

Preheat the oven to 220°C. Line a baking tray with non-stick baking paper. Place the flour and salt into a medium-sized mixing bowl. Add the olive oil and water then stir to combine with a fork. Transfer to a lightly floured surface and knead the dough together. Continue to knead the dough a further 5 minutes until it becomes smooth and elastic.

Roll the dough out to a 25cm square and place on the baking tray. With a knife, lightly score the surface of the dough to make 16 even squares. Brush well with pizza sauce leaving a half centimetre gap at the edges. Place a slice of pepperoni onto each square. Slice the olives and sprinkle over evenly. Cut each mozzarella ball into 4 rounds then place on top of the pepperoni. Bake for 8–10 minutes until the crust turns golden brown.

Serves 4

Dill & Crème Fraîche Scones

The subtle flavour of these savoury scones goes very well with salted or smoked fish like salmon, cod and caviar. I like to cut them small and use as canapés topped with extra crème fraîche and a dill sprig.

200g plain flour

2 teaspoons baking powder

½ teaspoon salt

1 small handful fresh dill leaves, chopped fine

200g crème fraîche

30mls water

Preheat the oven to 220°C. Sift the flour, baking powder and salt together into a medium-sized mixing bowl. Add dill and crème fraîche then work in with a fork until you have even-sized-looking clumps. Add the water and gently mix until only just combined.

Pour the mix out onto a floured workbench and knead until the dough just comes together. Dust again with flour and roll the mix flat with a rolling pin to 1cm thick. Cut out 4cm ovals with an oval cookie cutter and place on a lightly floured baking tray. Knead the offcuts gently back together and repeat the rolling and cutting process. Bake for 6–8 minutes until they are lightly browned.

Makes 20

Cheese & Onion Scones

Savoury scones pair ideally with soups, and cheesy scones are my favourite with pumpkin or root vegetable creamed soups. Cheese makes scones beautifully brown so don't be afraid to leave them in the oven a touch longer for a golden glow!

1 medium-sized onion, peeled

2 tablespoons soya bean oil

1 teaspoon caster sugar

200g plain flour

2 teaspoons baking powder

¼ teaspoon salt

100g feta, grated fine

100g ricotta

50g quality Parmesan, grated fine

125mls milk

Slice the onion in half through the core. Cut away core then slice thinly along the grain of the onion. Heat the oil gently in a medium-sized sauce-pant then add the onion. Stir on a medium heat until the onion begins to brown. Add the sugar and cook another 5 minutes, stirring occasionally – add 2 tablespoons water if the onion starts to stick. Cook approximately 5 more minutes or until browned and caramelised. Set aside to cool.

Preheat the oven to 220°C. Line a baking tray with non-stick baking paper. In a medium-sized mixing bowl, sift in the flour, baking powder and salt. Add the cooled onion, feta, ricotta and Parmesan. Add the milk and stir to combine with a fork.

Tip the dough onto a lightly floured surface and knead a couple of times to bring the dough together. Dust with flour then roll into a log around 4cm wide. Flatten log slightly then cut into 3cm slices. Place on the baking tray cut side up and bake for 7–9 minutes until golden brown and cooked through.

Makes 15

Double Cream Brie Scones

These mildly cheesy scones are surprisingly light and airy. They are perfect to accompany a cheeseboard and will match all cheese flavours, fruit pastes and chutneys. Perfect ending to a long lunch or dinner party!

200g plain flour
2 teaspoons baking powder
¼ teaspoon salt
100g Brie cheese, grated
200–250mls double cream

Preheat the oven to 220°C. Line a baking tray with non-stick baking paper. Sift the flour, baking powder and salt together into a medium-sized mixing bowl. Add the Brie cheese and 200mls cream. With a fork, mix until you have even-sized-looking clumps. If the mix is too dry to form dough, add the remaining 50mls cream and mix through.

Place on a floured workbench and knead a couple of times. Dust with flour and roll the mix flat with a rolling pin to 1cm thick. Cut out 5cm squares and place on the baking tray. Knead the offcuts gently back together and repeat the rolling and cutting process. Bake for 8–10 minutes until they have risen nicely and browned around the edges.

Makes 20

Whitebait Drop Scones

You can make a simple and tasty fritter mix with scone dough using half the flour you would for scones. With the addition of crème fraîche, the fritters fry deliciously crisp on the outside yet have a creamy-soft centre that doesn't overpower whitebait's gentle flavour.

100g plain flour

1 teaspoon baking powder

½ teaspoon salt

80g crème fraîche

zest of half a lemon

2 tablespoons flat leaf parsley, finely chopped

100–150mls water

100g whitebait

soya bean oil for frying

sea salt flakes

fresh lime wedges

Place a large cast-iron pan onto a medium heat. Sift the flour, baking powder and salt into a medium-sized mixing bowl. Add the crème fraîche, lemon zest, chopped parsley and 100mls water then whisk until smooth. Whisk in enough water to give the mix a "drop" consistency. Stir in the whitebait.

Drizzle around 2 tablespoons of oil into the hot pan. Making sure there is plenty of whitebait in each spoonful, drop 5 large tablespoons of batter into the pan. Leave to cook on a gentle heat for a couple of minutes. Turn over and leave in the pan until cooked through. Transfer to a warm oven to keep hot. Wipe the pan clean and drizzle in more oil. Repeat the process with the remaining batter. Serve warm with a sprinkle of sea salt and fresh lime wedges.

Makes 10

Sweet Scone Recipes

Cream Scones

If you ever wondered how professionals make such amazingly light scones for Devonshire tea, look no further. The secret is the cream scone recipe. Cream replaces butter *and* milk, and while you think this might make the cooked scone heavier, it doesn't. The dough is easy to roll out and form into shapes then cook into light, airy and simply superb scones.

200g self-raising flour
¼ teaspoon salt
50g caster sugar
200–250mls double cream

Preheat the oven to 220°C. Sift the flour and salt together into a medium-sized mixing bowl. Add the sugar and 200mls cream then work in with a fork until you have even-sized-looking clumps. If the mix is too dry, add the remaining 50mls cream and mix through.

Place on a floured workbench and knead a couple of times. Dust with flour and roll the mix flat with a rolling pin to 1cm thick. Cut out 5cm circles with a crimped circle cutter and place on a lightly floured baking tray. Knead the offcuts gently back together and repeat the rolling and cutting process. Bake for 6–8 minutes until they have risen nicely and browned around the edges. Serve with red fruit jams and extra whipped cream.

Makes 12

Crunchy Butter Scones

Its all very well coming up with innovative ideas for scone recipes, but many puritans are only interested in the classic-style – *moist and soft on the inside yet crunchy on the outside* – scone. Brushed egg is applied to the scones 10 minutes prior to cooking to achieve the "crunch". Because of this, don't use a buttermilk and soda recipe as the raising begins immediately when the dough is formed.

200g plain flour

2 teaspoons baking powder

¼ teaspoon salt

70g butter

50g caster sugar

50g sour cream

70–90mls milk

1 egg

additional tablespoon milk

Preheat the oven to 220°C. Sift the flour, baking powder and salt together into a medium-sized mixing bowl. Rub in the butter until it resembles fine breadcrumbs in texture. Add the sugar and sour cream then work in 70mls milk with a fork until you have even-sized-looking clumps. If the mix is too dry, add enough of the remaining milk to form dough.

Place on a floured workbench and knead minimally to bring together. Dust with flour and roll the mix flat with a rolling pin to 1cm thick. Cut out 5cm circles with a cookie cutter and place on a lightly floured baking tray. Knead the offcuts gently back together and repeat the rolling and cutting process. Whisk together the egg and tablespoon of milk. Brush the scones with the egg mix and leave to sit for 10 minutes. Bake for 6–8 minutes until they have risen nicely and browned around the edges. Serve with red fruit jams and extra whipped cream.

Makes 8

Banana & Yoghurt Griddle Cakes

Griddle cakes are superb for breakfast or brunch and the omission of butter makes this easy yummy recipe a little easier on the waistline.

250g self-raising flour
½ teaspoon salt
50g sugar
1 banana, peeled and mashed
250g thick Greek yoghurt
extra fresh banana
runny honey

Place a large cast-iron pan onto a medium heat. Sift the flour and salt into a medium-sized mixing bowl. Add the sugar, banana and yoghurt. With a fork, stir until the mix comes together to form dough.

On a floured surface, knead 2 or 3 times. Roll out until the dough is 1cm thick. Cut circles with an 8cm cookie cutter then re-roll the scraps and repeat the process until the dough is used up. In 2 batches, place the dough into the hot dry pan. Turn over after 2 minutes then cook a further 2 minutes. Serve 2 hot cakes per person with extra sliced fresh banana and runny honey.

Serves 4

Banana Bran Scones

These rustic treats are perfect for the kids' lunch boxes or that early-morning coffee break. Enjoy with a smear of soft butter or cottage cheese or they are just as good *au naturel*.

150g plain flour

50g bran

2 teaspoons baking powder

½ teaspoon cinnamon

¼ teaspoon salt

1 banana, peeled and mashed

100mls double cream

50mls apple juice

Preheat the oven to 220°C. Place the flour, bran, baking powder, cinnamon and salt into a medium-sized mixing bowl and stir together. Add the banana, cream and apple juice. With a fork, stir to combine then work into a dough with your hand. You may need a little water to moisten the dough if it is too dry.

Place the dough on a lightly floured surface and roll into a log 5cm wide. Slice into 14 even pieces and place on a lightly floured baking tray. Bake for 6–8 minutes until lightly browned and cooked through.

Makes 14

Lemon Scones with Curd

I love these elegant scones served with high tea or as petit fours. They are so beautiful and yummy to eat that they are deserving of your best china being pulled from storage to make an occasion of them.

250g plain flour

¾ teaspoon bicarbonate of soda

¼ teaspoon salt

50g caster sugar

75g butter

finely grated zest of 1 lemon

200mls buttermilk

lemon curd

soft whipped cream

Preheat the oven to 220°C. In a medium-sized mixing bowl, sift the flour, bicarbonate of soda and salt. Add the sugar. Rub in the butter until its texture resembles fine breadcrumbs. Add the zest and buttermilk then work the mix together gently with a fork. When almost combined, knead a couple of times with your hands to bring the dough together.

Tip out the dough onto a floured surface and roll out to a thickness of half a centimetre. Cut strips 3cm wide on an angle then cut dough on the opposite diagonal 3cm apart to create diamond-shaped scones. Transfer gently to a baking tray lined with non-stick baking paper. Bake for 5–6 minutes until lightly browned. Serve when cool topped with lemon curd and soft whipped cream.

Makes 25 petite scones

Sour Cream Griddle Scones

Scones were originally made on a cast-iron griddle and the dough cooks very quickly on a controlled low heat. These scones are a perfect breakfast treat smothered in maple syrup with lashings of soft butter. Their texture is airy light and they quite simply melt in your mouth.

250g plain flour

¾ teaspoon bicarbonate of soda

¾ teaspoon cream of tartar

½ teaspoon salt

50g sugar

75g butter

250g sour cream

¼ cup water

Place a large cast-iron pan onto a medium heat. Sift the flour, bicarbonate of soda, cream of tartar and salt into a medium-sized mixing bowl. Add the sugar. With your fingers, rub in the butter until it resembles fine breadcrumbs. Add the sour cream and work in with a fork. Add the water a little at a time until the mix comes together to form a dough – you may not need all the water.

On a floured surface, knead the dough 2 or 3 times. Divide into 2 then pat each into a flat circle around half a centimetre thick. Cut each circle into 6 wedges. In 2 batches, place the dough into the hot dry pan. Turn over after 2 minutes then cook a further 2 minutes. Serve hot with butter and golden syrup.

Serves 4

Almond Scones

Almond scones remind me of the simple home-cooked almond biscuits my mother used to make. They are a perfect afternoon snack with tea or coffee, and for an extra-special treat serve them with softened marzipan and whipped cream.

200g plain flour
2 teaspoons baking powder
¼ teaspoon salt
50g soft brown sugar
70g ground almonds
70g sliced almonds
200mls double cream
water

Preheat the oven to 220°C. Sift together into a medium-sized mixing bowl the flour, baking powder, salt and sugar. Add the ground and sliced almonds. With a fork, minimally work in the cream. Add a little water, just enough to bring the mix together into a dough. Knead 2 or 3 times then place dough on a lightly floured surface.

Roll out to a rectangle 30cm x 15cm. Slice off any uneven edges then slice into 4cm squares. Place on a lightly floured baking tray then bake 4–6 minutes until lightly browned and cooked through.

Makes 25

Brandy-Soaked Date Scones

While this recipe does require a small amount of preparation the day before, it is well worth the effort for the end result. Once the dates have been soaked the resulting scone is packed with delicious brandy-laced gooeyness! Serve these divine scones while still warm with red fruit jams and butter.

100g dates
60mls brandy
200g plain flour
2 teaspoons baking powder
¼ teaspoon salt
50g caster sugar
70mls double cream
70mls fresh orange juice, filtered

Slice the dates in half lengthways and remove the seeds. Place in a small mixing bowl and toss with the brandy. Cover and soak overnight.

Preheat the oven to 220°C and line a baking tray with non-stick baking paper. Sift the flour, baking powder and salt into a medium-sized mixing bowl. Add the dates plus any remaining brandy, sugar, cream and orange juice. Stir with a fork to combine.

Transfer to a lightly floured bench and knead a couple of times to bring the dough together. Roll into a 5cm wide log. Cut the dough with a sharp knife evenly into 8 pieces doing your best to keep the slices round in shape. Transfer to the baking tray cut side up and pat the dough a little so they sit flat. Bake for 8–10 minutes until lightly browned and cooked through.

Makes 8

Buttermilk Drop Scones

From breakfast to dessert, buttermilk drop scones are a versatile recipe you can enjoy with coffee and tea or as a meal before midday. And without the sugar and cinnamon they make a perfect savoury canapé topped with salted fish or caviar.

250g plain flour

¾ teaspoon bicarbonate of soda

½ teaspoon salt

50g sugar

75g butter

300mls buttermilk

cooking oil

1 tablespoon ground cinnamon

additional 50g sugar

Place a large cast-iron pan onto a medium heat. Sift the flour, bicarbonate of soda and salt into a medium-sized mixing bowl. Add the sugar. With your fingers, rub in the butter until it resembles fine breadcrumbs. Add the buttermilk and stir the ingredients together until just combined.

Lightly brush the pan with oil. Drop teaspoonfuls of batter into the pan. Leave to cook on a gentle heat for a couple of minutes. Turn over and leave in the pan until cooked through. Transfer to a warm oven to keep hot then repeat the process with the remaining batter. Mix together the cinnamon and sugar and pour into a small dipping bowl. Serve warm drop scones with the sugar and cinnamon on the side.

Makes 30

Rich Dark Chocolate Scones

Dark chocolate scones are divine served warm with soft whipped cream or try them with lashings of chocolate sauce and ice cream for dessert. This recipe works just as well with milk chocolate in place of the dark.

100mls double cream

60g dark chocolate

200g plain flour

2 teaspoons baking powder

¼ teaspoon salt

1 tablespoon cocoa

50g caster sugar

80–100mls water

Preheat the oven to 220°C. Pour the cream into a microwave-proof jug then break in the chocolate. Microwave for 1 minute on high. Stir the cream and melted chocolate until smooth. Set aside to cool to room temperature. Sift the flour, baking powder, salt and cocoa into a medium-sized mixing bowl and stir in the caster sugar. Pour in the cream mixture and mix minimally to combine. Stir in enough of the water to form dough. Transfer to a lightly floured surface and knead minimally to bring together.

Roll the dough out until half a centimetre thick. Cut out circles with a 5cm cookie cutter and place on a lightly floured baking tray. Roll the remaining dough out again and repeat the process. Bake in the oven for 6–8 minutes until browned around the edges and cooked through.

Makes 12

Cranberry & Greek Yoghurt Pinwheels

These fruity treats are perfect for people who don't like their sweets too sweet. The cranberries and yoghurt give a delightful tartness to these scones that matches perfectly with red fruit teas like guava and ruby grapefruit.

170g dried cranberries

300mls water

200g plain flour

2 teaspoons baking powder

¼ teaspoon salt

50g caster sugar

200g thick Greek yoghurt

water

extra caster sugar for dusting

Place the cranberries and water into a medium-sized sauce-pan. Bring to the boil then turn down to a simmer. On a gentle heat, reduce the liquid until it has evaporated. Set aside and leave to cool to room temperature. Preheat the oven to 220°C. Line a baking tray with non-stick baking paper then set aside. In a medium-sized mixing bowl, sift the flour, baking powder and salt. Add the sugar and yoghurt. Knead lightly into a dough – you may need to add a little water if the mix is too dry. Place the dough on a lightly floured surface. Roll out to a rectangle roughly 40cm x 25cm.

Place the dough on the bench so the 40cm length is horizontal. Sprinkle evenly with the cranberries. Brush the far edge lightly with water. Roll the dough up, rolling from the front to the back. Press lightly to make sure the sticky edge secures the roll. Slice into 12 rounds. Place slices cut side up onto the baking tray. Sprinkle lightly with extra sugar and bake for 6–8 minutes until lightly browned and cooked through.

Makes 12

Dairy-Free Scone Cake

If you are lactose intolerant or prefer to stay clear of dairy products, then this is the recipe for you. While I have served the dairy-free scone recipe as a cake, you can substitute the basic ingredients in most of the recipes in this book excluding those with cheese. While it has a slightly different flavour and texture, it will work as well baked in any shape, or recipe, as the dairy-based scones.

200g self-raising flour
¼ teaspoon salt
50g caster sugar
30mls soya bean oil
150mls soy milk
extra caster sugar for dusting

Preheat the oven to 220°C. Line a baking tray with non-stick baking paper. Place the flour and salt into a medium-sized mixing bowl. Add the caster sugar, oil and soy milk, then stir to combine with a fork. Transfer to a lightly floured surface and knead the dough a couple of times until it is just combined.

Roll the dough out to a 25cm square and place on the baking tray. With a knife, lightly score the surface of the dough to make 16 even squares. Dust well with sugar. Bake for 5-6 minutes until the cake puffs and turns light golden brown.

Serves 6

Green Tea Scones

The ultimate tea scone can be made with tea! While you can substitute green tea with Earl Grey or English Breakfast, green tea works super well, giving the scone an almost wholemeal colour and gentle flavour. Also, if you use vanilla essence or paste, be careful just to use a little as it can overpower the tea flavour. Green tea scones pair beautifully with fruit jams and sweet spicy fruit chutneys.

2 quality green tea bags

150mls boiling water

200g plain flour

2 teaspoons baking powder

¼ teaspoon salt

50g butter

50g caster sugar

1 scraped vanilla bean

Pour the water onto the tea bags and let them steep until the water is room temperature. Preheat oven to 220°C. Sift the flour, baking powder and salt into a medium-sized mixing bowl. Rub in the butter until you have the consistency of fine breadcrumbs. Add the sugar and vanilla. Squeeze out the tea bags and discard. With a fork, stir in enough green tea to form dough.

Place the dough on a floured workbench and knead a couple of times. Dust again with flour and roll the mix flat with a rolling pin to 1cm thick. Cut out 5cm circles with a round cookie cutter and place on a lightly floured baking tray. Knead the offcuts gently back together and repeat the rolling and cutting process. Bake for 6–8 minutes until lightly browned.

Makes 12

Gingerbread Scones

I love the flavour of gingerbread, but the cookies are so brittle, and a cake takes so long to cook! Here is the quick solution. Gingerbread scones are ready to eat in minutes, and while baking make the kitchen smell like Christmas! My favourite way to serve them is hot out of the oven, smothered in caramel sauce and vanilla ice cream.

200g plain flour

2 teaspoons bicarbonate of soda

¼ teaspoon salt

2 teaspoons ground ginger

½ teaspoon ground allspice

50g butter

50g caster sugar

50g treacle

150mls buttermilk

Preheat the oven to 220°C. Sift the flour, bicarbonate of soda, salt and spices into a medium-sized mixing bowl. Cut the butter into a fine dice and rub into the dry ingredients until it has the consistency of fine breadcrumbs. Stir in the sugar. Separately stir together the treacle with the buttermilk. Add the liquid to the dry ingredients. With a fork, stir to combine.

Transfer to a lightly floured surface and knead a couple of times to bring the dough together. Roll into a 10cm x 30cm rectangle. Slice into 20 even triangles. Transfer to a lightly floured baking tray and bake 5–7 minutes until the edges brown and the scones are cooked through.

Makes 20

Lemonade Scones

Lemonade scones are so well loved in New Zealand and Australia that if I didn't include a version of it, I expect people would write to me and complain. So here it is, for those who have never made them before and for the legion of fans who adore them. The recipe is quite standard but I have added a little lemon zest, and while this is optional, I feel it is a shame to have no lemon flavour considering the recipe's name.

200g self-raising flour
¼ teaspoon salt
25g caster sugar
1 teaspoon grated lemon zest (optional)
60mls double cream
lemonade (carbonated fizzy drink)

Preheat oven to 220°C. Sift the flour and salt into a medium-sized mixing bowl. With a fork, stir in the sugar, zest and cream. Stir in enough lemonade to form dough.

Pour the mix out onto a floured workbench and knead until the dough just comes together. Dust again with flour and roll the mix flat with a rolling pin to 1cm thick. Cut out 5cm circles with a round cookie cutter and place on a lightly floured baking tray. Knead the offcuts gently back together and repeat the rolling and cutting process. Bake for 6–8 minutes until lightly browned.

Makes 12

Mascarpone & Fig Scones

Mascarpone makes decadent scones delightfully light in colour and texture. Together with figs, these Italian-themed scones will impress guests and family alike for the few months when figs are in season. Serve these for a special occasion like a christening or a Sunday high tea.

200g plain flour

2 teaspoons baking powder

¼ teaspoon salt

50g caster sugar

200g mascarpone

¼ cup water

4 large figs

extra caster sugar for sprinkling

Preheat the oven to 220°C. Line a baking tray with non-stick baking paper. Sift the flour, baking powder and salt into a medium-sized mixing bowl. Add the sugar and mascarpone. With a fork, work the mascarpone into the dry ingredients until combined. Add the water then knead minimally into dough.

Place the dough onto a lightly floured surface. Roll out evenly to half a centimetre thick. Cut 5cm rounds from the dough with a cookie cutter and place on the baking tray. Place the scraps back together and roll out again, repeating the process until the dough is used up. Bake in the oven for 6–8 minutes until lightly browned and cooked through. Switch the oven to grill. Place a round of sliced fig onto each scone and sprinkle lightly with sugar. Grill for around a minute until all the sugar melts.

Makes 12

Mini Saffron Dampers

Dampers are an Australian, early settler version of scones. Damper dough is basically the same as scone dough but they were cooked in cast-iron pots over an open fire. This version uses saffron as a simple spice flavour and is lightly sweetened with sugar. Cut and shaped into mini dampers, they become sweet buns and can be served the same way.

30mls boiling water

1 large pinch saffron

400g plain flour

4 teaspoons baking powder

¼ teaspoon salt

100g caster sugar

100g butter

200–250mls buttermilk

extra buttermilk and caster sugar for glazing

Sprinkle the saffron over the water and leave to soak for 2 hours. Preheat the oven to 200°C. Line a baking tray with non-stick baking paper and set aside. Sift the flour, baking powder and salt into a medium-sized mixing bowl. Add the sugar. Rub in the butter until it resembles the texture of fine breadcrumbs. Add the saffron water and 200mls of the buttermilk then stir to combine with a fork. If the mix is too dry to form dough, add the remaining buttermilk.

Turn the dough out onto a floured workbench. Knead together until the dough becomes smooth on the surface. Cut the dough into 8 even pieces. Shape into round balls and place on the baking tray. Make 2 cuts in a cross pattern on top of the dough. Brush with extra buttermilk then sprinkle lightly with caster sugar. Bake for 15–20 minutes until they turn golden brown and sound hollow when tapped.

Makes 8

Passionfruit & Ricotta Scones

Using ricotta as an ingredient gives a scone an almost cake-like consistency, being slightly heavier than cream scones yet moist in texture. As a result, passionfruit and ricotta scones can ultimately be served as a delicious tea cake with lashings of clotted cream and extra fresh passionfruit.

200g plain flour

2 teaspoons baking powder

¼ teaspoon salt

85g caster sugar

125g ricotta

125mls fresh, scooped passionfruit

Preheat the oven to 220°C. Line a baking tray with non-stick baking paper. Sift the flour, baking powder and salt into a medium-sized mixing bowl. Add the sugar and ricotta. Stir to combine with a fork until you have even-looking clumps. Add the passionfruit and stir the mix until it begins to form dough.

Transfer to a lightly floured bench and knead a couple of times to bring the dough together. Roll into a 5cm wide log. Cut the dough with a sharp knife evenly into 8 pieces, doing your best to keep the dough round. Transfer to the baking tray and pat the dough a little so they sit flat. Bake for 8–10 minutes until lightly browned and cooked through.

Makes 8

Vanilla Bean & Mascarpone Scones

Mascarpone makes decadent scones that are delightfully pale in colour and texture. Delicately flavoured with vanilla bean, these gorgeous scones will impress guests and family alike. Serve for occasions like a christening and Sunday high tea or just as an extra-special treat.

200g plain flour

2 teaspoons baking powder

¼ teaspoon salt

50g caster sugar

½ teaspoon vanilla paste or 1 scraped vanilla bean

200g mascarpone

¼ cup water

sweetened, soft whipped cream for serving

fresh hulled strawberries

Preheat the oven to 220°C. Sift the flour, baking powder and salt into a medium-sized mixing bowl. Add the sugar, vanilla and mascarpone. With a fork, work the mascarpone into the dry ingredients until you have even-sized clumps. Sprinkle over the water then knead minimally into dough.

Place the dough onto a lightly floured surface. Roll out evenly to 1cm thick. Cut 5cm rounds from the dough with a cookie cutter and place on a lightly floured baking tray. Place the scraps back together and roll out again, repeating the process until the dough is used up. Bake in the oven for 6–8 minutes until lightly browned and cooked through. When cool, slice the scones in half through the middle and fill with whipped cream and strawberry slices.

Makes 15

Spiced Apple & Ricotta Pinwheels

I loved making Dutch apple cake as a child with plenty of lemon juice and spices. The recipe translates well to pinwheel scones and the addition of ricotta makes them extra scrummy!

200g plain flour

2 teaspoons baking powder

¼ teaspoon salt

50g caster sugar

150g ricotta

100–120mls milk

1 apple

2 tablespoons soft brown sugar

⅛ teaspoon ground nutmeg

¼ teaspoon ground cinnamon

zest and juice of 1 lemon

Preheat the oven to 200°C. Line a baking tray with non-stick baking paper then set aside. In a medium-sized mixing bowl, sift the flour, baking powder and salt. Add the sugar and ricotta. With a fork, work the ricotta into the flour. Add 100mls milk and knead lightly into a dough – you may need to add a little milk if the mix is too dry. Place the dough on a lightly floured surface. Roll out to a rectangle roughly 40cm x 25cm.

Place the dough on the bench so the 40cm length is horizontal. Peel the apple, slice into quarters and cut away the core. Cut into a small dice. Sprinkle the apple, brown sugar, spices, zest and juice evenly over the dough. Brush the far edge lightly with water. Roll the dough up, rolling from the front to the back. Press lightly to make sure the sticky edge secures the roll. Slice into 12 rounds. Place slices cut side up onto the baking tray. Bake for 10–12 minutes until lightly browned and cooked through.

Makes 12

Rosewater Scones

Perfect for a high tea or anniversary, rosewater scones are sugary sweet and delightful to eat!

200g plain flour

2 teaspoons baking powder

¼ teaspoon salt

50g caster sugar

200mls Greek yoghurt

40–60mls water

extra caster sugar for sprinkling

100mls double cream

1 tablespoon rosewater

2 roses

Preheat the oven to 220°C. Line a baking tray with non-stick baking paper. Sift the flour, baking powder and salt together into a medium-sized mixing bowl. Add the 50g sugar and yoghurt then work in with a fork until you have even-sized-looking clumps. Add enough of the water to form soft dough.

Place on a floured workbench and knead a couple of times. Dust with flour and roll the mix flat with a rolling pin to 1cm thick. Cut out 5cm hearts with a heart-shaped cookie cutter and place on the baking tray. Knead the offcuts gently back together and repeat the rolling and cutting process. Sprinkle lightly with extra caster sugar. Bake for 6–8 minutes until they have risen nicely and browned around the edges. Leave to cool to room temperature. Whip the cream and rosewater together until it forms soft peaks. Top the scones with rose whipped cream. Arrange picked petals on the cream. Serve immediately.

Makes 12

Rum & Raisin Squares

You can't go wrong with rum-soaked raisins in baking! I also added treacle and soft brown sugar to give these gorgeous scones a rich caramel flavour and colour. You just have to try them!

200g raisins
60mls dark rum
200g plain flour
2½ teaspoons baking powder
¼ teaspoon salt
30g soft brown sugar
50g treacle
100mls double cream

Place the raisins in a small mixing bowl and toss with the rum. Cover and soak overnight.

Preheat the oven to 220°C. Line a baking tray with non-stick baking paper. Sift the flour, baking powder and salt into a medium-sized mixing bowl. Add the sugar, treacle, raisins plus any remaining rum and cream. Stir with a fork to combine.

Transfer to a lightly floured bench and knead a couple of times to bring the dough together. Roll out to a rectangle 30cm x 15cm. Slice off any uneven edges then slice into 4cm squares. Place on the baking tray then bake 4–6 minutes until lightly browned and cooked through.

Makes 8

Whiskey Prune & Chocolate Scones

One of my favourite flavour combinations is brought together with whiskey-soaked prunes and chocolate chip scones. Texture is important with a scone like this so use succulent, sweet prunes and keep your chocolate chips chunky for the best results.

100g prunes

60mls whiskey

200g plain flour

2 teaspoons baking powder

¼ teaspoon salt

50g caster sugar

80g dark chocolate chopped roughly

½ teaspoon vanilla paste or 1 scraped vanilla bean

70mls double cream

70mls fresh orange juice, filtered

Slice the prunes in half and place in a small mixing bowl. Toss with the whiskey. Cover then soak overnight.

Preheat the oven to 220°C and line a baking tray with non-stick baking paper. Sift the flour, baking powder and salt into a medium-sized mixing bowl. Add the prunes plus any remaining whiskey. Add the sugar, chocolate, vanilla, cream and orange juice. Stir with a fork to combine.

Transfer to a lightly floured bench and knead a couple of times to bring the dough together. Roll into a 5cm wide log. Cut the dough with a sharp knife evenly into 12 pieces. Transfer to the baking tray cut side up and pat a little so they sit flat. Bake for 8–10 minutes until golden brown and cooked through.

Makes 12

Scone Biscotti

Biscotti is one of the most popular biscuits enjoyed internationally with coffee or tea. This recipe is a simple version of biscotti, made with scone dough. The result is a light and crisp biscuit that has a good shelf life of a week or two in an airtight container. Be sure to let the logs cool entirely before cutting and use a sharp serrated knife to minimise crumbling.

200g plain flour

2 teaspoons baking powder

1 pinch ground cinnamon

¼ teaspoon salt

85g caster sugar

50g butter

120g pistachios, unsalted

100–120mls milk

Preheat the oven to 200°C. Line a baking tray with non-stick baking paper and set aside. Sift the flour, baking powder, cinnamon and salt into a medium-sized mixing bowl. Add the sugar. Rub in the butter until it has the texture of fine breadcrumbs. Add the pistachios. With a fork, stir in enough milk to form dough.

Place onto a lightly floured workbench and knead together minimally. Divide the dough into 2, then roll each piece into a log 25cm long and 4cm wide. Place the logs onto the baking tray leaving plenty of space between them. Bake for 15–20 minutes until cooked through. Remove from the oven and turn the temperature down to 110°C. Let the logs cool, then with a fine-textured serrated knife, cut slices on an angle about 1cm thick. Place slices back onto the baking tray and bake 30 minutes. Leave to cool before removing from the tray.

Makes 20

Scone Doughnuts

Why make doughnuts with scone dough, you ask? Because it's quicker and easier! Enough said.

1 litre soya bean oil for deep frying

200g plain flour

½ teaspoon baking soda

¼ teaspoon bicarbonate of soda

¼ teaspoon salt

50g caster sugar

25g butter

100mls buttermilk

1 teaspoon ground cinnamon

¼ cup extra caster sugar for dipping

Pour the oil into a heavy-based sauce-pan and place on a low heat. Sift the flour, bicarbonate of soda, baking powder and salt together into a medium-sized mixing bowl. Stir in the sugar. Rub in the butter until it resembles the texture of fine breadcrumbs. Add the buttermilk and stir together with a fork until it forms dough. Knead together minimally then place on a lightly floured surface.

Roll out until the dough is evenly a half centimetre thick. With a 5cm circle cookie cutter, cut circles out of the dough. Knead scraps gently back together and repeat the process. Cut small holes in the centre of the circles. Place a scrap of dough into the oil to check it bubbles and is hot enough for frying. Fry dough rounds for around half a minute on each side until evenly browned. Drain on paper towels. Mix together cinnamon and remaining sugar. Dip doughnuts into the sugar mix while still warm and serve immediately.

Makes 12

Scottish Oat & Treacle Scones

This recipe is my version of the earliest leavened scone recipes known. Scones originated in Scotland and were oat based. Using treacle for the sweetener adds a caramel flavour and gorgeous golden colour to the scones. Enjoy them warm with butter on a cool winter's morning.

150g plain flour

3 teaspoons baking powder

¼ teaspoon salt

150g rolled oats

75mls double cream

75mls milk

75g treacle

Preheat the oven to 220°C. Sift the flour, baking powder and salt into a medium-sized mixing bowl. Add the rolled oats. Separately, whisk the cream, milk and treacle together until smooth. Add the liquid to the flour, and with a fork, work until almost combined.

On a floured surface, knead the dough 2 or 3 times to bring together. Divide into 2 then pat each into a flat circle around 15cm wide and 1cm thick. Cut each circle into 6 wedges. Place on a lightly floured baking tray. Bake for 6–8 minutes until they have risen and browned slightly.

Makes 12

Toffee Strawberry Scones

Toffee dipping is a little dangerous so always have ice water on hand. If the toffee touches any part of your skin, place in the water immediately.

200g plain flour
2 teaspoons baking powder
¼ teaspoon salt
50g caster sugar
100g mascarpone
100g plain yoghurt
water
100g extra caster sugar
60mls water
a few drops red food colouring
12 large strawberries

Preheat the oven to 220°C. In a medium-sized mixing bowl, sift the flour, baking powder and salt. Add the sugar, mascarpone and yoghurt. With a fork, stir minimally to combine. Knead lightly into a dough – you may need to add a little water if the mix is too dry.

Place the dough on a lightly floured surface. Roll out to half a centimetre thick. Using a 5cm circle cookie cutter, cut rounds from the dough and place onto a lightly floured baking tray. Bake for 6–8 minutes until lightly browned and cooked through.

Place the 100g caster sugar and water into a small high-sided saucepan. Stir to combine. Place on a medium heat and bring to the boil. Simmer until the caramel turns light brown then remove from the heat. Add the red food colouring and shake to mix through. Leave to cool a couple of minutes. Dip in the strawberries one at a time and place on top of each scone.

Makes 12

Toffee Dumplings

Nothing compares with sweet sticky dumplings on a cold winter's night! Toffee dumplings are essentially scone dough cooked in golden syrup. They have a gorgeous toffee flavour, and because they have been poached in cooking liquor they are super soft and airy light in texture.

80g soft brown sugar

160g golden syrup

325mls water

200g self-raising flour

¼ teaspoon salt

50g caster sugar

50g butter

125mls milk

Place the brown sugar, golden syrup and water into a medium-sized sauce–pan. Bring to a simmer then simmer for 5 minutes. Meanwhile, sift the flour and salt into a medium-sized mixing bowl. Add the sugar. Rub in the butter until the texture resembles fine breadcrumbs. With a fork, stir in the milk until just combined.

Transfer dough to a lightly floured surface. Knead a couple of times then roll into a log around 4cm wide and 25cm long. Slice into 12 even pieces. Roll into balls and place into the hot syrup, cover and turn the heat down to low. Cook for 20 minutes or until a skewer passed through the centre of a dumpling comes out clean. Serve hot with ice cream, whipped cream or hot custard.

Serves 6

Christmas Scone Cake

The smell of this cake baking will put you in the festive mood! The delicious spices and brandy-soaked fruit go down a treat with spiced eggnog on Christmas Eve or Christmas Day before the big dinner. Don't forget, while it is a cake, it is also a scone recipe, so enjoy it freshly baked and still warm.

8 dried figs

35g currants

60g raisins

60mls brandy

200g plain flour

2½ teaspoons baking powder

¼ teaspoon salt

50g caster sugar

1 teaspoon mixed spice

½ teaspoon ground cinnamon

50g glacé ginger, roughly chopped

200mls double cream

extra caster sugar for sprinkling

Cut the figs into 4 slices each and place in a small mixing bowl. Add the currants, raisins and brandy. Stir to combine, cover and chill overnight.

Preheat the oven to 200°C and line a baking tray with non-stick baking paper. Sift the flour, baking powder and salt into a medium-sized mixing bowl. Add the brandy-soaked fruit, sugar, mixed spice, cinnamon and glacé ginger. Stir the ingredients together with a fork then add the cream. Mix ingredients to form dough then transfer to a lightly floured workbench.

Knead the dough a couple of times then roll out to a 20cm round. Transfer to the baking tray. Score 8 wedges lightly across the surface. Bake for 15 minutes then sprinkle with extra caster sugar and bake a further 5 minutes. Serve warm slices with butter or brandy butter.

Makes 30

Glossary

Aioli
Garlic-flavoured home-made mayonnaise. Traditionally made with pounded roasted garlic and served on large thin croutons as an accompaniment to soups.

Baking powder
Leavening agent made from a combination of baking soda, tartaric acid and stabiliser.

Baking soda
Leavening agent that can be used in a dough or batter containing an acidic ingredient. One of the components of baking powder.

Buttermilk
Traditionally made from the liquid left over after churning butter from full cream milk. It is now more often made from skimmed milk, mixed with milk solids and cultured with lactic acid. You can make buttermilk by mixing 1 cup milk with 1 teaspoon lemon juice and leaving it to stand for 10 minutes.

Caster sugar
Fine white sugar.

Cornmeal
Flour ground from dried corn. It is available ground to fine, medium, and coarse consistencies.

Crème fraîche
French for "fresh cream". Originally produced in Normandy, a European version of sour cream but with less acidity and lighter texture.

Crimped cookie cutter
Cutter, usually circular, with ridged edge.

Ganache

Chocolate, butter and cream cooked together then chilled. Used as a base for chocolate truffles, cake glazes and piped cake garnishes.

Gluten

The mixture of proteins found in wheat grains, which are not soluble in water and that gives wheat dough its elastic texture. Baker's flour is high in gluten content while cake flour is low.

Griddle

A flat, heavy metal plate used for cooking, usually cast iron. In traditional cultures, the griddle may be a stone, brick slab or tablet. Used over an open flame, or on a stove, to cook many foods, with or without oil.

Kneading

To mix and work into a uniform mass with the hands.

Leaching

The action of passing water through wood ashes to extract the alkali.

Leavening

A substance used to make baked goods rise by the formation of gas, especially carbon dioxide, in the batter or dough, such as baking powder or yeast.

Light

Light refers to a recipe with less fat but should not be confused with low fat.

Marzipan

A paste made from pounded almonds and white sugar.

Mascarpone

An Italian method of making cream cheese that has a full cream flavour and softer texture in comparison to cream cheese.

Palette knife
A long thin paddle with handle made of flexible metal used for loosening dough from a floured surface.

Pearlash
An early form of leavener that works when mixed with an acidic ingredient in a batter or dough. The result of leaching via wood ashes.

Petit fours
Miniature desserts usually served with coffee at the end of a meal.

Pinwheels
Dough with or without filling rolled up and cut to create spiral-shaped baked goods.

Quick bread
Bread leavened with soda instead of yeast.

Raising agents
Leaveners used to make bread and baking double in volume, such as baking powder, soda and yeast.

Ricotta
A creamy curd made from whey, a by-product of cheese making. It is cooked twice which solidifies the albumin protein giving it a soft, cheese-like quality. The name ricotta literally means "re-cooked".

Self-raising flour
A blend of standard flour and baking powder.

Sifting
The passing of dry ingredients through a fine sieve to aerate and remove lumps.

Soda bread
Bread leavened with soda instead of yeast.

Sodium pyrophosphate
Stabiliser used in baking powder to stall leavening until the application of heat.

Unleavened
Baked goods, usually bread, made without a raising agent, such as flatbreads.

Vanilla bean
The seed pod of a vanilla plant derived from orchids. To use the pod, slice down its length and scrape out the seeds. The seed scrapings are the part you use to flavour recipes. The skins can be placed in an airtight container with caster sugar for vanilla sugar.

Vanilla paste
Made of the seeds which are still visible, vanilla paste is now widely available in supermarkets. This is a cheaper way to buy vanilla as the paste is strongly flavoured. You will only need to use a small amount to add a totally authentic vanilla flavour to a dish.

Whitebait
Whitebait are juvenile fish of the Common Galaxias species. They are caught and cooked en masse due to their small size – generally 5cm long and half a centimetre wide. Their flavour is extremely delicate and they are most commonly eaten in fritters.

Index

Conversion Chart

Measures

We use the following measures:
One metric measuring cup holds approximately 250ml; one metric tablespoon holds 15ml; one metric teaspoon holds 5ml.

The difference between one country's measuring cups and another is within a two or three teaspoon variance and will not affect your results.

All cup and spoon measurements are level. The most accurate way of measuring dry ingredients is to weigh them. When measuring liquids, use a clear glass or plastic jug with the metric markings.

We use large eggs with an average weight of 60g.

Liquid Measures

METRIC	IMPERIAL
30ml	1 fluid oz
60ml	2 fluid oz
100ml	3 fluid oz
125ml	4 fluid oz
150ml	5 fluid oz (¼ pint)
190ml	6 fluid oz
250ml	8 fluid oz
300ml	10 fluid oz (½ pint)
500ml	16 fluid oz
600ml	20 fluid oz (1 pint)
1000ml (1 litre)	1¾ pints

Dry Measures

METRIC	IMPERIAL
15g	½oz
30g	1oz
60g	2oz
90g	3oz
125g	4oz (¼lb)
155g	5oz
185g	6oz
220g	7oz
250g	8oz (½ lb)

Oven Temperatures

These oven temperatures are only a guide for conventional ovens. For fan-forced ovens, check the manufacturer's manual.

	C (CELCIUS)	F (FARENHEIT)	GAS MARK
Very slow	120	250	½
Low	150	275-300	1 - 2
Moderately low	160	325	3
Moderate	180	350-375	4 - 5
Moderately hot	200	400	6
Hot	220	425-450	7 - 8
Very hot	240	475	9

Length Measures

1cm	½in
2cm	¾in
2.5cm	1in
5cm	2in
6cm	2½in
8cm	3in
10cm	4in
13cm	5in
15cm	6in
18cm	7in
20cm	8in
23cm	9in
25cm	10in
28cm	11in
30cm	12in (1ft)

scones

First edition published by White Knights Publishing 2010
This UK edition published in 2010 by Accent Press Ltd,
The Old School, Upper High St, Bedlinog,
Mid-Glamorgan, CF46 6RY

The right of Genevieve Knights to be identified as the
author of this work in accordance with the Copyright,
Designs and Patents Act 1988 is hereby asserted.
Designed and typeset by Wayne Knights.
Edited by Mike Wagg.
Genevieve's portrait photographed by Anja Gallas.
Scones in History and Scone Secrets reference checked by
Jacquie Morris, Takapuna Library, Auckland.
Special thanks to Helen Woodhouse and the Takapuna
Library staff for all their support.

Printed and bound by Toppan Leefung Printing Limited, Hong Kong

ISBN 9781907016479

www.accentpress.co.uk
www.sconesbook.com
www.genevievescuisine.com